BBC MUSIC GUIDES

SCHUBERT SYMPHONIES

BBC MUSIC GUIDES

General editor: GERALD ABRAHAM

BBC MUSIC GUIDES

Schubert Symphonies

MAURICE J. E. BROWN

BRITISH BROADCASTING CORPORATION

Contents

Published by the British Broadcasting Corporation
35 Marylebone High Street, London W1M 4AA

SBN 563 10149 0
First published 1970
© Maurice J. E. Brown 1970

Printed in Great Britain by
Cox & Wyman Ltd, London, Reading and Fakenham

The First Six Symphonies

Very little has been written about Schubert's first six symphonies and this is understandable. It was not until broadcasting began to enrich the orchestral repertory to an undreamt-of extent that they emerged from the obscurity of printed full scores stacked on library shelves. For the modern music-lover Schubert's youthful symphonies entered the concert repertory in 1930 or thereabouts. Sir George Grove wrote a short description of these works and their manuscript scores which was published in 1869, and there was an admirable essay by Dvořák on the symphonies (quoted above), published in 1894; apart from these articles nearly all critical commentary has been written in the last forty years.

A common factor links these recent commentaries: the style of Schubert's early symphonies, we are told, is that of Haydn and Mozart. The remark, intended to be slightly dismissive, is in fact a rare tribute. And as far as Schubert's Fifth Symphony, in B flat, is concerned, to call this work Mozartian is to pay Mozart a compliment. These six symphonies remind us of the two older composers, and of Beethoven, because Schubert was speaking the same language as they, and speaking it as ably; but he was saying things in it so different from theirs that the six works are wholly typical of the young composer and of him alone.

From the first he was a master. Nothing in these six symphonies is immature, which is not to say that they are without flaw. The elementary factors, harmony, counterpoint, dynamic balance and so on, are assured and spontaneous; the melody is often enchanting and key-transitions are bold and original. Rhythmically, it can be admitted, Schubert shows a certain insensitivity. The rhythm of his themes has, occasionally, a fine sense of classical balance, but it is often square-cut and its repetitions lead to monotony. The rhythm of his structures, too, is inflexible; when one passage of tension and climax is followed by another, and yet another, as in the first movement of the *Tragic* Symphony, the effect is surely the opposite of what he must have intended. But the material, both thematic and structural, is in itself so attractive and so full of verve that the rhythmic weakness is overborne by the rich profusion of these musical offerings. Economy is, after all, the supreme achievement of the mature composer; in a young artist it would suggest poverty of invention. If Schubert's uneconomical outpouring in these early symphonies does show any lack of control, it is only in this indifference to rhythmic demands.

His orchestration in the six works has a sureness of touch and an appreciation of the beauty of instrumental colour which owed nothing to his predecessors. As a lad he played in, and conducted, the students' orchestra at the Vienna Konvikt (city college), of which he was a member for five years. The experience was of inestimable value, for, as William McNaught has said:

> Schubert learnt to orchestrate by playing in an orchestra; not a body of high-class professionals who could play any notes set before them, but a band of young players in whose hands any unsuitable or unpractical writing for instruments would betray itself.

The repertory of this college orchestra is not given fully in any of the memoirs of Schubert's friends. We are told only that they played symphonies by Haydn and Mozart (the latter's G minor Symphony being a particular favourite of Schubert's, something which we hardly need to be told) and the first two symphonies of Beethoven. In addition the symphonies and overtures of various lesser men such as Krommer, Kozeluch, Méhul and Weigl figured in their concerts. It was for this band of young players that Schubert wrote his first two symphonies and possibly his third. In all three works the orchestra comprises the usual strings and woodwind, with trumpets, horns and drums.

SYMPHONY NO. 1, IN D MAJOR (D.82)

The work was composed during the autumn of 1813, being completed on 28 October. Externally it has the pattern which Schubert, with only two modifications, was to follow in all six symphonies: a slow introduction to precede his first movement proper, a slow movement, a minuet and trio, a quick finale. In one feature of the formal layout he was a true innovator: he makes, in his First and Third Symphonies, the slow introduction a cohesive part of his first movement by reusing its material, in *allegro* tempo, to introduce his recapitulation or to furnish his coda. This device was not an isolated experiment, belonging only to these two early works. It recurs many times in his mature instrumental work, and examples can be found in the overture to *Alfonso und Estrella*, in the finale of the Octet and, most remarkably, in the first movement of the great C major Symphony.

The *adagio* introduction of the First Symphony is short, but its striding octaves have a noble air, besides performing their functional task of establishing the key of D major; the fortissimo opening shades down to a quiet cadence in A major and on this note of expectancy the first movement, an *allegro vivace*, makes an effective entry. The mood is of innocent happiness; whatever shadows may lurk beneath Schubert's sunny surfaces in later symphonies, there are none here. His first theme is little more than a decorated scale of D major and the subsequent orchestral chords are equally lacking in any melodic significance. But his second theme is a different matter. Above a dancing accompaniment the violins play this delicious Viennese song:

Ex. 1

Too much has been made of the chance resemblance between the phrases in bars 2 and 4 and those of Beethoven's *Prometheus* tune. More interesting is the consideration of another comparison between the two composers which Schubert's theme conveniently touches off. Beethoven's use of the short, striking thematic figure with which to erect his miracles of symphonic structure was, during the nineteenth century, accepted as essentially the right way; Schubert's sustained, lyrical themes were held to be incapable of such intellectual treatment. To hold this view is conveniently to overlook these two factors: the vitality of Schubert's melodies and a true understanding of what is meant, *in music*, by the term 'intellectual'. Intellectual power in a composer's music is not indicative of a powerful intellect, using the word in its accepted application to mean other, non-musical aspects of man's thought; one has only to think of Bach or Beethoven to see the force of this assertion. Schubert's intellectual power, and that of the other half-dozen or so great composers, is shown in the way that chosen themes pervade the thought and saturate every bar of the symphonic movement; nor, in Schubert's case, need we look for it only in the big instrumental movements, for it is found in his songs and smaller pianoforte works to an equal degree. As for his partiality for the lyrical subject-theme, he has his own ways of using this too, and one of them can be seen in connection with the melody quoted above. After its soft unfolding, first by the strings and then by the woodwind, the full orchestra takes it up thus:

Ex. 2

The cadential figure *a* adds all the thrust and vigour which are required to enable the composer to write a splendidly direct, original and forceful development section – and its composer was sixteen years old! It is far and away the finest movement he had composed until then, and it remained unequalled in his instrumental output until the finale of the Second Symphony composed some eighteen months later. The return of the *adagio* introduction at the end of the development section throws some light on the problem of what Schubert intended by the term *vivace*. In my opinion it is to be interpreted as indicating mood rather than speed; many of his movements marked *vivace* cannot make their full effect if they are played too quickly, e.g. the finale of the A minor Sonata (D.845). The *adagio* section of the First Symphony, when it returns, is given doubled note-values in the *allegro vivace* tempo; this implies that the composer thought of the quicker tempo as twice the speed of the slower one, which, in the case of this movement at least, does not justify equating *vivace* with 'very quick'.

The only other instrumental works that Schubert composed at this period were string quartets. The *andante* of the First Symphony, 6/8 in G major, resembles the slow movements of the string quartets as closely as they resemble one another. Schubert seems content to establish a contemplative mood, touched with a slight melancholy, in which the melodies (which only just pass muster) succeed each other and recur in the right formal places, and the whole progress is leisurely and almost undistinguished. When such a mood and such a succession of melodies are composed with awakened genius the result is the slow movement of the Fifth Symphony; the *andante* of the First Symphony is workmanlike and pleasant, but apart from one passage it gives no hint of what Schubert will do with this type of movement later on. The passage occurs in bar 23 when the opening melody has finished its course. The music moves into E minor; the rising phrases of the oboe and the repeated string chords are to reappear, and with more Schubertian individuality, in the Fifth Symphony movement.

The minuetto is perfection. The opening phrases combine melody, harmonic sequence and a bold rhythm in so accomplished a fashion that one would be hard put to it to say which of the three was the dominating idea in the composer's mind. The short, sinuous quaver-figure at the cadence is seized upon and provides the interest of the middle section. There are touches of the Beethoven scherzo here, but they are too slight to affect the general impression of a true minuet. The trio is an early example of Schubert's 'rustic dance-tune' which occurs frequently in this contrasting section of his third movements, even as late as the G major Sonata of 1826. The melody is played by violins and bassoons in octaves, a touch of orchestral colour to which Schubert was partial; before the reprise of the melody the high woodwind utters little ejaculatory phrases which tell us very plainly of Schubert's love for Mozart's G minor Symphony.

The manuscript of this Symphony carries one or two revisions which show pretty clearly that the young composer heard it rehearsed and performed: most of them occur in the finale and were undertaken to simplify the string accompaniments. This is understandable, for, as Richard Capell said, if music wants to race it must strip: Schubert's rondo-finale is one burst of joyous and racy sound, and the original triplet runs on the strings are almost unmanageable at the speed demanded by the music. The opening theme is twofold. A tripping melody on the violins, lightly accompanied, is paired with a more substantial theme given out by the full orchestra:

Ex. 3

The second section is a long dissertation on a single theme; it starts with the little figure marked *b* in Ex. 3(i) which reminds us of the trio theme. Schubert uses his theme with much ingenuity; it is played pianissimo on the woodwind against held, chromatic chords on the strings; it is used as a canon between flute and violins against clarinet and oboe; it is given full orchestral harmonies. All the while the key-colours fluctuate between D major, D minor and F major. But as Dvořák has said in his essay:

> If Schubert's [early] symphonies have a serious fault it is prolixity; he does not know when to stop . . .

The opening section reappears, changed only in details of modulation, and this is followed by the second section, reduced to half its original length. The coda is short, and the introduction of a new rhythm, using a triplet figure, is a grateful contrast. This device was inspired by the finale of Beethoven's C minor Symphony and produces a similar effect of peroration.

SYMPHONY NO. 2, IN B FLAT (D.125)

During the year which elapsed between the finishing of the First Symphony and the beginning of the Second, Schubert composed forty or so works. Among them are three string quartets, two of which, in E flat and B flat, are in the concert repertory. There are two full-scale works, the three-act opera *Des Teufels Lustschloss* and his first Mass, in F major. There is also a group of songs, including 'Gretchen am Spinnrade'. Such a body of work, giving him experience in all spheres of composition, was bound to have its effect on his symphonic writing and the greater power is obvious at once. There is no gain in authority – that was revealed to the full in the First Symphony – but the invention is more individual and the handling of modulation and harmonic resource is markedly freer.

Sir Donald Tovey's famous essay on Schubert's tonality, published in *Music & Letters* for October 1928, brought about the same revelation in Schubert scholarship as Caroline Spurgeon's even more famous essay on Shakespeare's imagery did for studies in his works. Subsequent scholars have taken the study of Shakespeare's imagery to excessive lengths, and perhaps there is a danger that the same thing is happening with studies of Schubert's tonality. That Schubert's response to key-colours, individual and collective, is without precedent, no one would deny. But that his instrumental movements, consciously and throughout, exploit definite tonal schemes is a little hard to swallow. The fascination of Schubert's tonality lies in the fact that his many so-called modulations do not depart from his fundamental key so much as emphasise its potentialities. The beginnings of his delight in these colourful and emotional effects of changing keys are found in his Second Symphony.

Schubert began the first movement of the work on 10 December 1814 and finished it in sixteen days. It starts with a short *largo*, a matter of ten bars, whose only feature of interest is a touch of instrumental felicity when high flute phrases alternate with pizzicato bass strings. The *allegro vivace* begins with a swift-footed theme which is later modified in a highly ingenious way; the theme and its pendant are shown here:

Ex. 4

(i) Allegro vivace

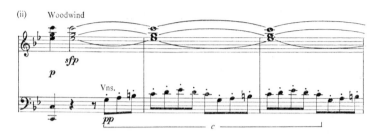

(ii) Woodwind

The phrase marked *c* is used with much resource and its possibilities were seen and appreciated by the composer, for it became the basis for his development section.

The second subject is in E flat. Classical convention requires that this subject should be in the dominant key, i.e. since Schubert's main key is B flat, his second subject should be in F major. This convention is, by Beethoven and Schubert, more honoured in the breach than in the observance, but however unconventional Schubert may be in the choice of key for his second subject he invariably concluded the section in the dominant and did so even to the very last works he wrote. The E flat melody is constructed, as is so often the case with his themes, on a succession of 'horizontalised' common chords of his key.

Ex. 5

The outline of this melody recurs, transfigured, in the second subject of the composer's celebrated *Quartettsatz*, the String

Quartet-movement in C minor, of six years later. The theme leads to a massive orchestral crescendo with hints of the rhythm and the bass-phrases of Ex. 4(ii), until a cadence in the conventional F major is reached. And here we encounter one of Schubert's serious miscalculations, one which has, doubtless, prevented this symphony from receiving the acclaim it deserves. He wrote a long passage, fortissimo, with almost unrestrained use of the full orchestra, based on the main theme in Ex. 4(i). This prolongs the exposition section to an almost unendurable extent and seriously upsets the hitherto perfect balance of the movement. He finally reaches the development section in bar 267. This section is a beautiful piece of writing. Above a running quaver bass, derived from the figure in Ex. 4(ii), slow, delicate melodic phrases on violins, flute, oboe and clarinet are woven together; D flat and its related keys persist throughout the episode until a quiet cadence in E flat brings us to the recapitulation.

Conventionally, a recapitulation should begin in the key of the movement. Here and elsewhere Schubert departs from convention by using his subdominant key. When this fact is commented on we read that he does it to save himself the trouble of modulating, since his second subject will automatically appear in the main key of the movement. And so it would if Schubert were always conventional in matters of key-choice. If, in this movement, he were trying to save himself the trouble of modulating, his second subject would appear in A flat. The whole recapitulation is recast and the composer has gone to a great deal of unnecessary trouble by his unconventional choice of key. The recapitulation follows its predestined course, even to a repetition of the long codetta.

The second movement is a theme and variations, the only example in Schubert of this form in orchestral guise. A song-like theme in E flat, marked *andante*, is followed by five variations and a coda. The melody is demure, the variations are unclouded, and they are scored with a light, sure hand. No great variety of mood is attempted; in the first three variations the theme is decorated by running quaver-figures in the bass or treble. The accompaniment takes on a more vigorous, triplet form in the fourth variation, but the relaxed mood is soon re-established for the fifth variation and the quiet, valedictory coda.

The minuetto – a scherzo in all but name – is an *allegro vivace* in C minor. Its striking theme was obviously inspired by the famous C major section of the scherzo in Beethoven's C minor Symphony. Schubert does not adopt the older composer's gruffness, nor his humorous breaks in the theme, but the development section continues the same on-running and ceaseless manipulation of the theme as in the Beethoven passage. The trio melody, in E flat, might be a sixth variation of the *andante* theme in the slow movement. The interest is enhanced with imitations between flute, oboe and clarinet and the subdued tone of the section is in marked contrast to the stormy nature of the minuet, all the more telling when it returns.

The finale, a *presto* in 2/4, is one of the finest movements in all six of the symphonies. It is beautifully constructed, a perfect fusion of rondo and sonata-form. The three-sectional movement has the following pattern:

A:B:A:: C ::A:B:A

The heart of the movement, C, is a full development of the first theme, A:

Ex. 6

Its treatment leads to an exuberant passage, almost free of modulation, except for the concluding move into E flat for the second theme. This is another and characteristic example of Schubert's early thematic styles: a succession of crisp fragments like mosaic chips whose design is not obvious until they are all assembled. The melody having been presented we have, suddenly as it were, the Schubert of the future unmistakably taking over, and for the first time in his symphonic progress. String octaves sink down from E flat to B flat and a powerful, highly chromatic passage is let loose in the orchestra. The first theme returns but this too is in the hands of an inspired Schubert and undergoes new and interesting modifications. The middle section is built entirely on a harmonic treatment of the opening four notes of the main theme, marked *x* in Ex. 6. The crotchet-quavers rhythm is drummed out in every bar; the clash in semitones resolves into remote keys. At first the orchestration is of chamber-music proportions, violins and oboes; gradually the rest of the woodwind enters, the bass strings, the horns, and with the entry of trumpets and drums the music hammers at the rhythm with fortissimo strokes. Not even Beethoven contented himself with iron rations such as Schubert chooses to furnish in this development section and with them prepare such a feast of good things. The dynamic eases and eventually reaches the opening cadence in B flat for the re-capitulation. It is a splendidly written movement, unequalled in originality among the works of his youth.

SYMPHONY NO. 3, IN D MAJOR (D.200)

This, the shortest of the first three symphonies, was started on 24 May 1815, but after the composition of the *adagio maestoso* introduc-tion and a few pages of the first movement, the score was set aside for several weeks. Work was resumed on 11 July and the rest of the symphony completed in eight days. The *maestoso* prelude aims at little more than establishing the key of D, but it contains an ascending-scale figure which Schubert introduces into the *allegro con brio* which follows. The instrumentation of the opening theme, as can be seen from his manuscript, caused him some trouble; originally scored for oboe and horns, then for strings, it finally reached its present form. The crisp, rhythmic figure for the clarinet alternates with string passages, and the mood is of Viennese gaiety. The ascending-scale figure, played by the full orchestra, preserves the high spirits and enables Schubert to build up to a climax; this, in characteristic fashion, breaks off suddenly. After a space of silence the second subject is played. As with many of his second subjects, it suggests spontaneous composition with the outlines of the first subject still running in his mind. The mood and style are thereby preserved but contrast is lacking. The development section is based on a short figure which might be derived from either of the two main subjects since its rhythm and shape are found in both. It is treated with much orchestral in-genuity and the tonal plan is masterly. F major is succeeded by G minor and by similar steps G minor leads to A minor. This is theorising, but the effect on the ear is deeply satisfying. In addition, Schubert the craftsman, aware of the insubstantial nature of his short thematic figure, introduces a sustained phrase in crotchets which cements the coruscating elements of his music together and eventually leads back to a fairly regular recapitulation. The coda is constructed on the scale figure of the *maestoso* introduction.

Schubert's manuscript shows that his original intention was to compose an *adagio* for his slow movement and that he actually jotted down a theme in this tempo. But it was abandoned and instead of looking back to Beethoven he looked forward (to Brahms?) and composed an intermezzo in G major marked *allegretto*. It is a delightful movement, childlike and innocent in melody and treatment. We can pay tribute to a young composer who could so completely put aside any attempt at elaboration and display, and write as his heart dictated. The great Schubert is glimpsed for a moment halfway through the movement, when a slower melody streams out on the violins.*

The third movement is a minuetto marked *vivace*. As in the Second Symphony, the style is purely that of a scherzo. The short theme is announced by the full orchestra in unison. It was mentioned above how frequently these themes of Schubert's are melodically based on a succession of tonic and dominant chords of the key. The minuet theme is quoted here since it provides an obvious example of this mannerism of the composer's theme-construction which occurs throughout his work, both instrumental and vocal. It can, in subsequent pages, be denoted as the 'tonic-dominant' pattern.

Ex. 7

The quiet violin figure which links the two halves of the theme is also characteristic of the procedure. The middle section is built entirely on the opening thematic fragment, and provides an apt

* A mistake which has crept into all editions of the symphony might be mentioned here. The opening section of sixteen bars in this *allegretto* is not marked for repeat in Schubert's manuscript. The error is rectified in the edition of the *Neue Schubert Ausgabe*, ed. Arnold Feil and Christa Landon (Tübingen, 1968).

illustration of Schubert's tonal experiments. The key is A major: the music passes through A minor, C major, D minor and B flat major before it returns to A major for the recapitulation of the opening bars. Before Tovey's essay, and Harold Truscott's subsequent development of its ideas,* this passage would have been considered one of free, even uncontrolled, modulation; the modern view would regard it as a composer's exploration of tonal regions which are all part of an A major tract. The trio is a gem of Schubertian melody, a near relative of the similar section in the First Symphony but more graceful in outline and more wistful in its appeal.

The Symphony closes with a finale marked *presto vivace* in 6/8. A first quick glance through its pages suggests a thinly scored tarantella, without much substance or contrast and without any sizeable melodic qualities. A second glance, however, reveals several highly successful rhythmic climaxes, a remarkable continuity with an underpinning of attractive and logical harmonic sequences. And as we look deeper the exuberance, the control of the material, the unflagging drive of the music bring about a revision of first judgements. In fact, in performance the movement is a superb experience. It is a complete refutation of the equating of sonata-form with solemnity, of the idea that genius is revealed only when it plumbs the depths or storms the heights. Schubert's ode to joy is in this finale, and it is the forerunner of those mature finales to the D minor String Quartet and the great C major Symphony.

SYMPHONY NO. 4, IN C MINOR ('TRAGIC') (D.417)

A glance at Deutsch's catalogue numbers† shows that Schubert composed something like two hundred works between his Third and Fourth Symphonies. The Mass No. 3, in B flat, two operettas, including the ill-fated *Claudine von Villa Bella*, the three sonatas for pianoforte and violin, the String Quartet in E major, many of his popular dances for the pianoforte, and a great number of songs,

---

* *The Symphony*, (i) *Haydn to Dvořák* (Pelican Books, London, 1966), pp. 188 *et seq.*

† *Schubert: Thematic Catalogue of all his Works* (Dent, 1951).

including the 'Erlkönig', were all completed by April 1816 when he turned to the composition of his C minor Symphony. School-days were over. If the symphony were performed at all, it was not by the students' orchestra of his college, but by a private orchestral society which had had its origins in the string quartet formed by the Schubert family.

The subtitle *Tragic* has given rise to a good deal of comment, usually drawing attention to its inaptness. Although Schubert's Symphony is in a minor key and, on occasion, adopts a grave tone of voice, it never takes the shape of drama; it evolves from its thematic material by purely musical processes. Schubert added the word *Tragische* to his manuscript some time after the Symphony was finished. Does this suggest anything of signifi-cance? We might perhaps conclude that the impulse behind his music was not, at first, formulated as tragic. This subtitling of one of his works in classical sonata form is a remarkable event; he did it on this occasion for the first and only time. Several of his youthful manuscripts, however, bear distinctly humorous, even schoolboyishly flippant, comments. The strangest occurs on the manuscript of the *Funeral Music*, D.79; the words 'Franz Schuberts Begräbnis-Feier' are, as Dr Fritz Racek has pointed out,* in the composer's own hand – 'Franz Schubert's Funeral' – and the piece probably marked his 'demise' as a scholar at the Vienna Konvikt. Yet no one, listening to that music, would consider it as other than a genuinely solemn funeral march. Is *Tragische* another of Schubert's humorous, or ironic, comments, marking perhaps with a rueful pen the tragic failure of its performance at the hands of the private orchestral society? The suggestion is far-fetched and possibly quite uncongenial to the reader, but if there is any validity in it at all it would at least remove the tendency to 'blow up the material beyond its natural limits' as one critic said after a grandiose performance of the Symphony. For the title raised hopes in the nineteenth century that Schubert was taking the right step – a step in the direction of Beethoven – and the hopes were bound to be dashed if Beethovenian standards are applied to this sym-phony of Schubert's. Taken on his terms, however, the four movements provide unalloyed pleasure to the listener, and it is

* *Festschrift zum hundertjährigen Bestehen der Wiener Stadtbibliothek* (Vienna, 1956), p. 115.

preferable when we listen to them to forget all about the *Tragic* of the title.

The introduction, *adagio molto*, is the longest, most substantial and far and away the finest, in these early symphonies. The theme is played on the strings, with exchanges between first violins and cellos.

Ex. 8

The figure marked *d*, although part of the sequential nature of the theme, is treated as a separate thematic unit and leads to a fortissimo close on a chord of G flat major. In this key the same canonic treatment of the theme occurs, magnificently handled, and passing through a web of *Tristan*-like harmonies to a cadence in C minor. Oboe and violins utter the figure *d* like an impassioned cry, before the music sinks quietly to a half-close in the initial key of the movement.

The *allegro vivace* begins at once with the main theme:

Ex. 9

Its sprightly nature cannot be disguised by any attempt at a solemn interpretation and its construction, based on the rising thirds, adds to the optimistic mood of the melody. Harold Truscott has drawn attention* to the close resemblance between the

Loc. cit. p. 193.

contours of the theme and that of the first movement of Beethoven's String Quartet in the same key (Op. 18, no. 4), but Schubert had his own methods of dealing with this melody and they are unlike Beethoven's. The announcement of his theme being accomplished, he wrote an energetic passage whose material derives from the three rising thirds of his main theme and which continues the confident mood of the opening:

Ex. 10

This figure finally modulates to A flat for the second theme, one of his lyrical outpourings of great charm. It leads to a further example of those upthrusting thirds which were used in the First Symphony; commencing in A flat they reach an orchestral tutti in E major. The passage is repeated and reaches its inevitable close in C major. Yet again the music is repeated and so comes full circle to A flat. This stepping downwards from one key to another a third below is common in Schubert but never commonplace, although he rarely uses it quite so baldly as here. Of more interest than this key sequence is the fact that we have here one of the earliest examples of a constructional feature which recurs in his instrumental work: the threefold presentation of material. In this case no overall tension is built up since the rise in excitement exists in each of the three sections, but it is otherwise in later work. The codetta presents more new material, which may derive from the very opening phrase of his main theme; whether or not, it is in keeping with the tone of the music and offers no marked contrast.

The development is a short and pithy dissertation on the main theme, introduced by fortissimo octaves on strings and woodwind; they have some of the gruff humour of Beethoven and suggest a series of false starts. The theme is then played in B flat minor and after an effective episode of imitation between bass and treble the cadence comes in G minor. In this instance Schubert was possibly seeking to save himself some trouble by beginning the regular recapitulation in that key, for his second subject does automatically appear in the orthodox key of E flat. There are changes towards the end, however, and the movement ends triumphantly in C major.

The slow movement is an *andante* in A flat. On the whole it is the most Schubertian, most lovable, of all the movements in the first six symphonies. It was, significantly, the only one of those movements to be published in score before Breitkopf & Härtel printed all the symphonies. The *andante* appeared from the firm of Peters in 1871. Had Schubert's intention been to compose a *Tragic* Symphony, here, in his slow movement, we should surely have had its deepest feelings. But the tone is that of nostalgia rather than grieving; the touch of Schubertian pathos is there, but never a hint of tragedy.

The melody is similar to one in his later work, the Impromptu in the same key, Op. 142, no. 2, and the gentle, timeless process is the same in both compositions. The form of this lyrical movement is that of a rondo. The second episode starts in F minor with a figure of accompaniment which sounds as if it is going to burst out into the main theme of the first movement, but the melodic phrases of the woodwind restore the serene mood of the opening. These phrases are of Schubert's 'mosaic' construction, but they cohere eventually into a sustained and lovely melody played by clarinet and flute over a throbbing figure on the strings. This ostinato figure gradually, but inexorably, mounts through the violin registers, never more than pianissimo, but by its persistent upward climb emerging to the foreground of the music. In a sensitive performance the effect can be enchanting. A feature of Schubert's later slow movements is found in this one: accompanying material from the second, contrasting episode is maintained in the recapitulation of the first section: the ostinato figure continues briefly as the main theme returns. In the later repetitions of the two sections, this accompaniment is further prolonged, pervading the whole of the final appearance of the opening melody until the coda. In the closing bars a change into triplets is introduced, a welcome rhythmic contrast, and the movement ends with a long diminuendo to *ppp*.

When we reach Schubert's minuetto and trio any idea of tragedy is meaningless: there is nothing in the music except the skilful presentation of fertile ideas – happy ideas, too, however chromatic and forceful the orchestral voices may be. The theme, far removed from the elegance and simplicity of the eighteenth-century minuet-tune, is played in unison by strings and woodwind:

Ex. 11

To seek in this symphony deliberate cyclic processes, i.e. the use of thematic ideas which the movements have in common, is possibly misguided, save for the fact that Schubert was by no means averse to this device. The themes of all the movements, for example, use the falling semitone with which the minuet tune opens; the anacrusis of the main theme of the first movement appears in the slow movement, in the trio melody, and again in the finale; the phrase marked *e* in Ex. 11 is an obvious reference to the striking progression in the *adagio molto* introduction. This phrase is the substantial element in the course of the minuet, and from it the composer evolves not only powerful harmonic progressions, but some individual and appealing melodies. The clashes in the harmony are managed with skill; typical of the composer in their astringency we find them throughout his scherzo-movements – at their finest in the C major String Quintet. The trio is yet another of the plaintive lyrical episodes he used for this part of the third movement: the true Schubertian tenderness and compassion shine clearly in the central cadence.

The finale, *allegro*, is an extended movement in sonata-form. The profuse material, endlessly inventive, can be reduced to two basic themes; these are developed in melodic, that is, in linear fashion. They are given with various figured accompaniments and these, too, sometimes emerge into prominence. The effect of the movement is of one long, lyrical effusion. The main theme, with its important derivative theme, together with the second subject, are as follows:

Ex. 12

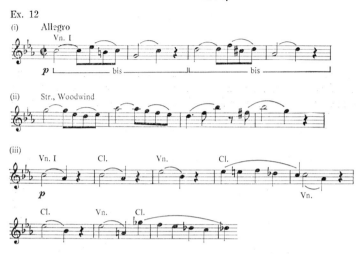

The mosaic-type theme in Ex. 12(iii) is a charmingly contrasted melody, but its rather fussy accompaniment is obtrusive and the staccato string notes cannot be subdued in performance. The codetta is based on (ii), to which the anacrusis from the first movement is added, and is given much prominence. The development section begins with an original and, tonally, arresting passage: it consists of the threefold presentation of an idea based on a juxtaposition of (i) and (ii). Each presentation starts with an octave figure on the strings and these sink through a minor third – D flat, C flat and B flat. The chromatic key-changes are bold, but the effect is perfectly logical and the use of the main theme gives a stable centre to the wheeling harmonies. These eventually reach A major and in this key an attractive and tuneful variant of (ii) is played successively by the various woodwind instruments. The music, aided by syncopated string octaves, builds up to a climax with full orchestral power and then subsides to a cadence in C major. The recapitulation begins in this key and the whole of the material from the opening of the movement is transposed into the major for this purpose. The second subject appearing in F major, no further modification is necessary, and the finale of Schubert's *Tragic* Symphony ends with confidence in that most optimistic of keys – C major.

SYMPHONY NO. 5, IN B FLAT MAJOR (D.485)

Schubert's Fifth Symphony occupies a unique position both in the symphonic work of his youth and in the affections of music-lovers. It is the shortest of the six and was written for an orchestra of almost chamber-music proportions: strings, one flute, two oboes, two bassoons and two horns. It was known in the nineteenth century as the 'Symphony without trumpets and drums', but the absence of clarinets is just as noteworthy. The score probably indicates the constitution of the private society at the time when he wrote the Symphony. It was composed during September and October 1816 and performed shortly afterwards.

In the four preceding symphonies there are several instances where Schubert's abundant flow of ideas led him to overlook points of formal construction; there are none in the Fifth Symphony. A notable aspect of the work, in theme and structure, is his sense of balance – the classical impulse which is never far from his creative thought. The spontaneous ease with which this music unfolds should not inhibit an appreciation of the beauty of design, the conscious artistry which has weighed and considered the importance of every musical element and its contribution to the whole conception – melody, harmony, orchestration and constructional development. The first movement, *allegro*, opens with the main theme. Commentators frequently describe these first five bars as an introduction to the theme which leaps into life in the fifth bar; but Schubert's intention can be seen if his development section is considered. A necessary digression here will illuminate his procedure at this vital point of sonata-form. In general, Schubert begins his first movements with the main theme. He composed, in round figures, seventy 'first' movements and there are four, possibly five, exceptions to this rule, the most prominent being that in the String Quintet of 1828. The main theme, sometimes of a preludial nature, is frequently followed by an energetic melody which serves to further the course of the exposition section and it may also recur in the development section; an example of this procedure can be found in the String Quartet in G (D.887). This artistic feature of his work may have been born in the First Symphony, when to the lyrical theme quoted in Ex. 1 he appended the lively, rhythmic figure which served his purpose so well in the development section. The point is that whatever immediate prominence he gives to a subsidiary theme he may, later on, ignore it entirely; but with the few exceptions mentioned his opening bars, containing the main theme, are never ignored. The point holds with this Fifth Symphony movement.

Ex. 13

The woodwind chords, with the tripping violin figure, are followed by one of his most attractive subsidiary themes built, once again, on the common chords of his key. This pendant theme forms the basis of a buoyant passage, full of youthful optimism; it bursts into an orchestral tutti like a triumphant hymn, a confident assertion that God's in His Heaven, all's right with the world. A short break and the strings announce the second subject, an admirably constructed and appealing melody. Having run its course, it concludes with cadential phrases which hover between F minor and F major with an ease and daring which are almost unbelievable for its period.

The development section starts with a consideration of the main theme. The woodwind chords are transferred to the strings; the tripping figure is still played by the violins and a counterpoint is added by flutes and oboes:

Ex. 14

A cadence is reached in E flat minor and the figure marked *x* dominates the scene. A tense climax is built up. In the slow relaxation which follows, the figure *y* on the oboes is the fundamental motive. The long, scaling-down passage leads to the end of the section. Another Schubertian feature is found here: the omission of his main theme in order to start his recapitulation with the bolder, subsidiary theme. The device was used on several subsequent occasions, for example in the *Unfinished* Symphony, and in the C minor Quartet-movement. The coda is formed from upward-rushing scales which end the movement on an exuberant note.

The *andante con moto* in E flat major is based on a song-like theme, and a series of after-phrases, with all the grace and sweetness which we associate with the young Schubert. It calls to mind the earlier songs of the *Schöne Müllerin* cycle and, like them, paints in incomparable fashion the peace and beauty of a pastoral summer's evening. A simple modulation which, in Schubert's hands, is of the essence of poetry, leads to the second subject. The first section ended in E flat: the orchestra climbs a chord of F flat and reaches C flat major. It is the composer's favourite drop from one key to another a third below, but never before or after this was the change made so magically. The second subject, even lovelier than the first, is a duet between strings and woodwind. It concludes with a long, and carefully worked, pattern based on that 'rising-thirds' figure which has appeared, in embryo, in earlier symphonies. All the material is now recapitulated with conventional key-changes, and a short coda completes this supremely accomplished movement.

The composer still calls his third movement a minuet, but actually the *allegro molto* is an out-and-out scherzo. The key, G minor, was used only in the instrumental movements of his youth, and always finds him in a masculine, aggressive mood. There are moments of gentler emotion in the course of the minuet but the general tone is fiery. The trio turns into G major and the melody has the pure, serene expression of the smaller songs he wrote at this time. The contrasting phrases at the heart of the trio are deceptively simple: there is a craftsman of great technical skill at work in their devising.

In the finale, *allegro vivace*, Schubert returns to the happiness and bounding delight of the first movement. As in the finale of his Third Symphony, we have a movement composed with simplicity of means and lightness of texture. But the melodies in this later finale are more tuneful, less figured; the points of repose are more cunningly placed; the sheer technical brilliance of his thematic development is admirable. The movement is in sonata-form and opens with the strings playing the main subject, one of Schubert's typically youthful B flat tunes:

Ex. 15

Contrast is provided by a figure which climbs in measured fashion the chords of G flat and D flat with full orchestral colouring; rapid string passages add to the excitement which culminates on a fortissimo cadence in F minor. There is a short silence and the second theme, in F major, is played by the strings. No more attractive melody can be found in his early symphonic music than this theme, graceful in contour and with a sustained lyricism in which Schubert is incomparable. The development section is a substantial episode founded on the initial phrase of the opening theme. There is a splendid use of contrapuntal exchanges between strings and woodwind and the keys darken to A flat and D flat. An intermediate section uses, once again, those chains of rising thirds which played so important a part in the slow movement. A new thematic idea is evolved which still shows its kinship with the basic motive:

Ex. 16

The gradual return to the recapitulation has no feature of outstanding interest except that it gives an impression of masterly control; there is no hint of a young composer's feeling that, since he has answered the demands of a technically brilliant development, he can bring back the recapitulation with a sense of having done his duty. Schubert moves with the ease and assurance of inexhaustible genius to the chosen moment for the return of his opening themes. Necessary key changes modify the recapitulation but they also re-create the freshness of the exposition. The impression left as the movement closes is that no more captivating finale could have been devised for this delightful work.

The first public performance of Schubert's Fifth Symphony took place on 17 October 1841 in the Josefstädter Theater, Vienna, conducted by Michael Leitermayer.*

SYMPHONY NO. 6, IN C MAJOR (D.589)

The year that elapsed between the conclusion of the Fifth Symphony and the commencement of the Sixth was an eventful one in Schubert's life; it was at this period that he first abandoned a regular teaching position in his father's school and launched out on his own with the intention of establishing himself as a freelance composer. It was eventful, too, in his inner creative life. The many compositions of the period include six pianoforte sonatas and about sixty songs; among those songs are many on which his fame is securely grounded – 'Der Wanderer', 'Der Tod und das Mädchen', 'An die Musik' and 'Die Forelle'. Such an enriching phase of his life would, one imagines, produce in his next symphony profounder depths of feeling and an even more adventurous handling of material and the orchestral medium. Such imaginings are vain; the Symphony is the least compelling of the six. The reason can be found in passage after passage throughout the work; Schubert is writing against the grain, trying to be, not himself, but Rossini. During 1817 the Italian's operas, fresh from their success in Naples, were produced in Vienna and received with frenzied enthusiasm. In other circumstances Rossini's music would not have had such an impact on Schubert, but he had just begun to try to earn a living and here – in this lightly melodious, sparkling music – seemed the secret of success.

* Information kindly supplied by the great Schubert scholar, Ignaz Weinmann.

His two overtures known as 'in the Italian style' belong to the same months as the Sixth Symphony; in fact, he must have worked on all three orchestral pieces turn and turn about. The themes of all four symphony movements are flimsy to the point of triviality and although he cannot be other than a fine craftsman in their presentation and treatment, this material is against him. Only in the scherzo does the real Schubert take control and his genius burns brightly for a brief while.

This Symphony has divided critical opinion more sharply than any of his others:

The work is a little gem and ... those who have heard Beecham conduct it will not take kindly to hearing it abused.
(Geoffrey Sharp)

This is a good symphony that happens to be extremely pretty, often in a prettified way; and if such a thing is a rarity it is not because any rule forbids it but because nobody else has had the gift to bring it off.

(William McNaught)

... Is the succession of charming little tunes known as Schubert's sixth symphony a festival work? Not, I grieve to say, for me. ... When one knows in advance exactly what will happen four bars hence, eight bars, sixteen, twenty-four, the suspense of waiting for the expected becomes positively nerve-racking.

(Ernest Newman)

Schubert began to compose the Symphony in October 1817 but it was not finished until the following February. He had been obliged to return to teaching at this period; his sense of failure and his unhappiness at the resumption of such daily tedium may account for the unusually long time which he spent on the work. The *adagio* introduction sounds like a first draft for the corresponding section of the 'Italian' overture in D major; this is well-known to music lovers since Schubert used it again for the *Rosamunde* overture. In the Symphony it raises expectancy and establishes the key of C major, but does little else. The *allegro* opens with a cheerful wisp of a tune (i) and who could possibly foresee that, eleven years later, exactly the same musical impulse would produce the opening theme of the String Quintet in the same key (ii)?

Ex. 17

The *allegro* proceeds by exploiting the various ingredients of the main theme and adds several Rossini-like tonic and dominant cadences. The second subject is also Italianate, preserving the mood of the foregoing material and adding a welcome fluidity to the music:

Ex. 18

The passage which follows this theme is full of colour and vivacity, using figure *c* in Ex. 18 with admirable resource. It becomes charmingly tuneful when the composer reaches the destined key of G major and the two phrases *a* and *b* in Ex. 17 are combined with it. This fusion of the second subject with motives from the first gives Schubert his material for the development section. The instrumentation, consisting of exchanges between solo woodwind and strings, is in his well-known 'conversational' style. The pure form of the main theme is finally treated in a softer, more flowing style; the key is E flat major and the return to C major for the recapitulation is a truly Schubertian stroke.

Ex. 19

The use of the descent through a third in the bass of this extract becomes more and more frequent in his work until the final miracles of the Great C major Symphony. The coda is much longer than hitherto in these first movements; it is marked *più moto*. This novel feature brings the movement to an end with a good deal of bustle and noise, and places it in the same category as the 'Italian' overtures which were its contemporaries.

The *andante*, in F major, is almost devoid of those touches of poetry and harmonic imagination which give such delight in the slow movements of the Fourth and Fifth Symphonies. It is, for Schubert, a sentimental movement, based on an uncharacteristic theme. This is quoted here in order to draw attention to a feature which is not native to the composer but inspired by his imitation of Rossini:

Ex. 20

The use of the semiquaver breaks in the third bar of the melody aims at a lilting effect and the device recurs at intervals throughout the movement. The contrasting section uses a triplet rhythm which, once it appears, is all-pervasive.

Schubert calls his third movement a scherzo for the first time in his symphonies although he had already used the form in a few chamber-music works of the previous months. It is a spirited movement; rhythmic figures melt into melodies which skim fleetfooted over the drumming bass-notes of pizzicato strings. Another novel feature of this third movement is the presence of an uninspired trio. It is more ambitious, more extensively planned, than its predecessors, but one regrets the composer's abandonment of his usual practice – to pen a melodious and unpretentious lyric at this point of his third movement.

The chief interest of the finale lies in the prophetic hint which it gives of the finale of the great C major Symphony. A rhythmic figure, almost the same as that which opens the later finale, occurs in the movement and forms the basis of the coda: it is as if this motive lay dormant in Schubert's mind until he eventually realised its potentialities and exploited them in the spring of 1828. Otherwise the themes of the finale are either insubstantial or untypically pretty and at no point are they woven into the fabric of the music. They are simply accompanied tunes.

When Schubert's Sixth Symphony is deemed to be less worthy than the preceding five, because in three of its movements at least he is adopting the pose and manner of Rossini, this is not, in any way, to belittle the charm and endearing vivacity of the Italian composer. 'How dull is the Mozartian idiom,' wrote Eric Blom, 'when Mozart is absent!' and the words apply equally well here. Rossini's idiom, with Rossini absent, is, even in Schubert's hands, unsuccessful.

Two Symphonic Fragments

The month in which Schubert finished his Sixth Symphony, February 1818, marks the end of his confident youth, the end of a period of ceaseless composition in which work after work had been brought to a successful conclusion. Before that date it is rare to find him embarking on a sonata, string quartet or symphony without accomplishing his task. But this confidence became undermined with doubt and uncertainty. The catalogue of his compositions between February 1818 and February 1823 is punctuated by unfinished and abandoned work; whatever external reasons can be found for this, the internal reason is obvious. In his instrumental music Schubert was trying to reconcile the thought of his mature genius with the youthful language which was no longer capable of expressing it. His vocal works – songs, part-songs and operas – did not pose quite the same problem, for the weight of tradition was not so heavy there, and he had, in any case, long before this found himself in song.

The conflict is most apparent in that form which is at the farthest remove from song; his work for two abandoned symphonies presents in an acute form the hopeless struggle to use the language of the six symphonies of his youth in which to express the deeper thoughts of his maturer years. The first of these (D.615) attempts dates from May 1818. The manuscript consists of thirty-four pages (seventeen leaves) of which twenty-five are filled with closely-written music. The material is written in pianoforte score so that these twenty-five pages represent an enormous amount of work. The key is, once again, D major. In all, Schubert sketched eight movements in this manuscript; the keys of them are all related to D major and one after the other was relinquished in his efforts to find a movement which satisfied him. The first sketch in the manuscript is for the conventional 'first movement', the second for the slow movement; after this there is a series of fragmentary movements composed with no ordered scheme in mind. They can, however, be grouped into the four-movement scheme of the classical symphony as follows:

I. *Adagio*, in D minor, 2/2; *allegro moderato*, D major, 2/2.
II. (*a*) D major, 2/4,
    (*b*) *andante*, B minor, 3/8,
    (*c*) A major, 2/4.
III. Scherzo, D major and Trio, G major, 3/4.
IV. Finale:
    (*a*) D major, 4/4, with two further variants,
    (*b*) D major, 2/4, with two further variants,
    (*c*) D major, 2/4.

The *adagio* introduction is a highly-chromatic improvisation; it reveals Schubert, with uncontrolled fancy, letting his motives and rhythms take what path they will. A long-drawn cadence in D minor concludes the section and then the *allegro moderato* begins, pianissimo, in D major. Only the exposition is sketched. The

c

themes are tuneful but characterless; the string figures which link them have a certain fluency and colour, but the style is still trammelled with Italianate elements. Although the section is thinly sketched right to the double bar, Schubert's interest had evidently long vanished. All three slow movements have more character. The first is Schubert in lyrical vein, with touches of poetry evoked by the simplest means, but the result, had he completed it, would have been no more ambitious than the *allegretto* of the Third Symphony. The *andante* in B minor is by far the most intriguing movement in the whole of the sketches. It is complete in all but a few details.*

The mood foreshadows that of the first movement of the *Unfinished* Symphony and there are episodes of touching poetry of the same essence as those in the slow movement of that Symphony. The third sketched movement, in A major, is a return to the simplicity of the first.

The scherzo and trio are traced in the barest outline. As they stand they are almost negligible, but one thing is certain: it is impossible to judge from Schubert's preliminary sketches by what incredible strokes he will elevate ordinary ideas. It has been said often, and with justification, that Schubert never composed a weak scherzo. Neither these sketches, nor those for the corresponding movement of the *Unfinished* Symphony, tell the full tale.

His seven attempts to compose a finale embody a vast amount of work which both awes and depresses. It goes a long way towards substantiating the idea put forward above, that he was a composer at odds with himself. The material is that of his boyhood finales, but it was no longer the kind of material that satisfied him or gave full expression to what he wanted to say. Here is the start of the second variant of his first finale:

Ex. 21

* It was performed for the first time, arranged by the present writer from the pianoforte score, on the BBC Third Programme, 23 November 1957. The pianist was Frederick Stone.

The third bar, hinting strongly at the theme of the unfinished Sonata in C major of 1825, might have led to a solid and satisfying stretch of work but it, together with the rest of the material, is soon submerged under a sea of scales and triplet-rhythms; these were delightful in the finale of the Third Symphony but here they are sterile. Further efforts to compose a finale were equally unproductive. In one of them Schubert resorts to a fugal exposition – which indicates the extent of his desperate need for stimulus. These sketches were preserved by the Schubert family and purchased from them by Nicolaus Dumba in 1883; he bequeathed them to the Vienna City Library. Whether they will ever be printed is doubtful; if they are, they would throw a fascinating light on Schubert's creative processes. They also suggest that in this manner he sketched all his symphonies and only when a symphony was successfully completed were the sketches destroyed.

It was perhaps a departure from this usual custom which led to the fragmentary state in which the second of his symphonic sketches (D.729) has remained. The manuscript consists of 147 pages ruled for a full score. The first twenty contain an *adagio* introduction in E minor and seventy-five bars of the succeeding *allegro* in E major complete in all details. From then onwards the symphony was composed, as a sketch, with Schubert thinking straight on to the paper. Every bar contains some indication of the continuity of the music and this holds good right to the end of the finale, where Schubert wrote, with a flourish, 'Fine'. Long stretches of each movement are indicated simply by the violin or flute part, even if, to judge by the fortissimo marking, music for the whole orchestra was in Schubert's mind. Other episodes are more detailed, with melody, accompaniment figures and bass clearly filled in. It was a bold venture and reading through these pages one gets the impression of a composer handling the orchestra, almost improvising on it, with an accomplished and perfectly assured touch. But Schubert must have known that it would not do, and the work is left in its fragmentary state because it was not the kind of symphony he felt impelled to finish. For consider its date of composition: August 1821. By that time he had composed the A major Piano Sonata (D.664), the *Trout* Quintet, the String Quartet-movement in C minor, to say nothing of the music for the melodrama *Die Zauberharfe*, or the Easter cantata *Lazarus*.

Schubert uses a bigger orchestra for this Symphony, asking for the same forces as he had been using in his operatic scores of the period. Trombones are found in his symphonic score for the first time. The *adagio* is a thoughtful and well-planned section based on the opening motive; this has two individual features, the slow theme on the clarinets, with an accompaniment for pizzicato strings:

Ex. 22

Both are separately developed, the bass figure in bar one receiving especially detailed attention. The introduction is thirty-four bars long, almost exactly the same length as that in the work sketched in 1818; both are more extended than any in the five early symphonies. The *adagio* ends in E minor with the horns holding, pianissimo, the dominant B. On this note of expectancy the *allegro* trips in. The chord of E major patters away on the lower strings and the violins enter with this theme:

Ex. 23

It is a winning little tune and in the first two or three symphonies would have been perfectly in place, but compare it with the themes which open the *Trout* Quintet, the A major Sonata, and the C minor Quartet-movement, and one might well wonder what on earth Schubert was about when he reverted to this eighteenth-century elegance in a new symphony. The theme is melodically treated and its light quality determines the style of the first part of the exposition. A figure on the clarinet, formed from a leaping octave phrase, is original and Schubert evidently intended to keep this promising idea up his sleeve for future use: it does recur later on, but not to the extent that it might have done had he completed the movement. A long bridge-passage eventually reaches B major and again the horns sound a sustained B.

The second subject, played by the clarinet, enters abruptly in G major. It is one of Schubert's simple tunes, moving step-wise, which can be touched with magic; this one is not. The music eventually reaches C major and the main theme returns in this key. Schubert now develops this theme, and its passing through remote keys and the build-up of tension are characteristic. But at the end of the section the second subject appears in E major, obviously as a resumption of the recapitulation. We are left in doubt as to which part of the movement Schubert has omitted. Is the episode starting in C major a true development, or is it the return of a modified exposition? When the symphony was first performed, on 5 May 1883, completed by J. F. Barnett, Sir George Grove wrote a programme note for the occasion. He remarked that neither in the first movement nor in the last did the main theme return in the regular manner of a formal recapitulation and added: 'Can it have been that a feeling that he had erred in this way wearied Schubert with his work and forbad his returning to it to complete it?' It is a shrewd suggestion, and together with a general dissatisfaction on Schubert's part probably represents the truth of the matter. The movement ends with a long coda based on new treatment of the main theme. This is certainly a fresh departure and signifies the maturing outlook of the composer. The coda emphasises the martial character of his theme, so that the movement ends in the style of a *marche militaire*.

The *andante*, in A major, has the same improvisatory character as some of the sketches for the 1818 movements. The melody is of secondary value, but it has a certain grace, and the falling thirds, marked *x* in the quotation, give it the nature of a cradle-song:

Ex. 24

All the themes of this E minor Symphony have a singular feature in common, illustrated by this quotation: it is the repetition of a short motive within the melody. This upsets the rhythmic balance although it avoids the charge of squareness. Schubert was very taken with the falling thirds in the marked phrases; practically the whole of the *andante* is based on them. Interest is maintained by the evolution of fresh melodies from the basic idea, by the transitions from key to key, and by the use of lyrical exchanges between various solo woodwind. But the movement languishes; it lacks contrast, especially the kind which would be generated by a subject fundamentally different from the opening lullaby.

The swinging C major tune which opens the scherzo initiates a movement having much in common with the scherzo of the Sixth Symphony. The music is too skeletal for us to assess its ultimate value: we cannot tell what the composer would have made of it. What Schubertian stroke, for example, was in his mind when, in the midst of an episode in C major, he gives the violins a long trill on A flat below the treble stave? Nothing else is written in the score at this point. The trio, in A major, again offers no contrast, seeming to be merely an extension of the rhythm and melodic features of the scherzo.

The finale, *allegro giusto*, is the most promising of the four movements. Its opening theme is as juvenile as that of the first movement, having, in fact, even less appeal. But its course being run, a second theme, in marked contrast and touched with the true Schubertian glow, takes over. It is based on the composer's earlier 'mosaic' style and its passage between the instruments, with never-failing invention, recalls the *andante* of the *Tragic* Symphony. The movement is in sonata form and the development section uses both the main themes. The recapitulation is anything but regular, being full of freshly composed passages. The final coda, too, has one or two fascinating new points. One of these is an original use of the syncopated accompaniment from the beginning of the movement.

Two men have attempted to fill in Schubert's score and so make a performance possible. J. F. Barnett's version has been mentioned; it was performed at the Crystal Palace concerts. In 1934 Felix Weingartner also completed the work. His version was performed in Vienna on 9 December 1934 and broadcast by the BBC on 27 March 1935. Both versions have been published – Barnett's only in piano score (Breitkopf & Härtel, c. 1884) – but Schubert's sketches are unprinted and so remain inaccessible except to a student of his manuscript. This was given by Ferdinand Schubert to Mendelssohn in 1845; after Mendelssohn's death, his brother Paul gave it to Sir George Grove, who bequeathed the score to the Royal College of Music. It is now in the British Museum.

Neither of the completions has succeeded in establishing the Symphony in the concert repertory and this is not to be regretted. Schubert has clearly indicated the form of his movements and his melodies, but harmonic details, accompaniment figures and cadences, are anything but clearly indicated and it is in these essential features that Schubert's magic chiefly lies. Barnett and Weingartner brought to bear on their tasks a useful knowledge of the Schubertian idiom and at this crux or that the solution of one or the other is admirable. But each version is inevitably a distorted or at least a partial Schubert, and better no Schubert at all than that.

The 'Unfinished' Symphony

A month after the composition of the sketch for the Symphony in E, Schubert left Vienna in the company of an intimate friend, Franz von Schober. They sought the peace and seclusion of a small residence at St Pölten, and their object was to work together on a three-act opera. This was *Alfonso und Estrella* and it occupied Schubert for the next five months, the work being completed at the end of February 1822. The experience was invaluable – so invaluable that in the autumn of that year a miracle happened. He turned once again to the composition of a symphony and this time he achieved that perfect fusion between thought and expression towards which he had been so painfully struggling. More than that, the conception, and the exquisite musical language in which it is embodied, was the most elevated and poetical he had attained. In Grove's famous phrase '... all trace of his pre-decessors is gone' and, we could add, all trace of his own preceding symphonies; in this Symphony in B minor, Schubert composed so novel and so sublime a work that even today it still holds at its heart the tantalising enigma of creative genius – how could a human mind conceive this music? Like all truly great works of art it contains that which lies beyond our senses and baffles our powers of understanding.

The Symphony is unfinished but not in the same way that the two previous symphonies are unfinished. On this occasion Schubert sketched in piano score the first three movements of his Symphony and then wrote, in fair copy, the full score of the first two. He began to score the third movement and then gave up his task. There is a world of difference between the manuscript of the Symphony in E, which is in Schubert's sketchbook hand, and that of the two fully-scored movements of the *Unfinished* Symphony; these are beautifully penned. Why did he give up the task of completing this symphony? The question has been asked repeatedly for over a hundred years, and it cannot be satisfactorily answered.

Schubert gave the manuscript to Josef Hüttenbrenner at some time during 1823, on the understanding that it would be passed on to his friend Anselm, Josef's older brother. Practically the whole edifice of biographical surmise which has been built up on this fact is slowly crumbling away under the impact of newly discovered documents and authentic disclosures from the descendants of Anselm Hüttenbrenner. There is no space here to deal with this complicated matter but from one charge Anselm Hütten-brenner can be absolved. The theory that Schubert sent him a complete symphony score from which he lost the scherzo and finale has been finally routed by a remarkable discovery recently made by Dr Christa Landon in Vienna.* She unearthed a quantity of autograph manuscripts which had passed from Schubert's posthumous papers into the possession of Kreissle von Hellborn, the composer's first biographer. Among them is the second page of the orchestral score of the scherzo of the Symphony. It is un-finished, showing that Schubert did not continue the full scoring

* See *Österreichische Musikzeitschrift*, May–June 1969, p. 299.

of this movement beyond the first page and that he himself removed the second page before handing over the score to Josef (he could not remove the first page, since this was written on the back of the last page of the *andante con moto*). The score of the *Unfinished* Symphony was given by Anselm Hüttenbrenner in May 1865 to Johann Herbeck, conductor of the orchestra of the Vienna Gesellschaft der Musikfreunde; the work was first performed, under Herbeck's direction, on 17 December 1865 and published in Vienna a year later. It was first performed in London at the Crystal Palace Concerts under the direction of August Manns on 6 April 1867. Some twenty years passed, incidentally, before the name 'Unfinished' became internationally bestowed on the work.*

There is no slow introduction and the first movement, *allegro moderato*, begins at once with the main theme. This famous melody, with its solemn, almost foreboding, air, is played in unison by cellos and double-basses, pianissimo. It is an opening unlike that of any other symphony in its modest, yet compelling, appeal to the ear. Nothing could be less like the arresting opening of the eight Beethoven symphonies which were composed before the *Unfinished* yet, by the strangest coincidence, the older composer's Ninth Symphony, on which he was working almost at the same time as Schubert was composing the *Unfinished*, opens with the same quiet, foreboding air. Schubert's theme is quoted here in order to draw attention to its construction:

Ex. 25

It is a succession of three two-bar motives as can be seen, first, by Schubert's phrasing and second, by the fact that he develops each of the motives separately. In performance it would be slightly precious to emphasise the correct phrasing, but that does not excuse the wrong phrasing, so frequently heard, whereby the theme is divided at the end of the third bar, with a slight em-

* On the long-perpetuated textual errors in practically all published scores, see Adam Carse, 'Editing Schubert's Unfinished Symphony', *Musical Times*, Vol. 95 (1954), p. 143.

phasis at the start of the fourth. An extremely attractive, figurative accompaniment follows on the violins, and clarinet and oboe in unison then play their slow cantilena – Schubert's subsidiary theme by which he intends to proceed with his exposition. The cadences are enforced by horns and trombones using a falling semitone derived from the phrase *c* in Ex. 25. This falling semitone might be considered a characteristic feature of the first movement but it is, in truth, a characteristic feature of the whole of the music of Schubert's maturity. The music of this section is radiantly lyrical, urged forward with growing tension to a climax of syncopated chords on a cadence in B minor. Horns and bassoons sustain the note D and this leads the music, by an unexpected cadence, into G major. An exactly similar device can be found, at the same formal point, in the String Quintet of 1828 and the outcome in both Symphony and Quintet is the same: one of Schubert's heaven-sent inspirations follows the abrupt transition. In the Symphony movement a syncopated accompaniment is played on basses, clarinets and violas and the cellos sing one of Schubert's most celebrated melodies:

Ex. 26

This is repeated by the violins and leads to a tremendous orchestral passage; it concludes with hammered chords which finish abruptly and leave the woodwind whispering the syncopated chords of the second subject. Against this background, phrases from the heart of the melody (*e* in Ex. 26) are treated in imitation by the string orchestra, first legato and then, with power and authority, in staccato octaves. A second huge climax is built up and again it gives way to the syncopated chords, this time on the strings. Schubert then takes the opening phrases of his second subject (Ex. 26 *d*) and evolves from them another episode of imitative exchanges between strings and wood; it is a bewitching passage and repeated hearings do not dim its freshness and charm. One of the extraordinary signs of Schubert's new maturity in this movement is the controlled economy by which he achieves his

effects. The soft, lyrical episodes and the massive orchestral out-
bursts are no longer protracted by the profusion of his ideas; they
are short, and all the more telling for being so.

The exposition ends with a bridge-passage as effective as it is
simple: the note B is sustained on woodwind and horns, while
pizzicato string octaves steer the music into B minor for the repeat
of the exposition. This convention of sonata-form was strictly
observed by Schubert throughout his life – mechanically so; in
many, if not in all, of his first movements, the repetition of the
exposition section is a duty which might well be abrogated. In the
first movement of the *Unfinished* Symphony, for example, to repeat
the exposition is to destroy the balance of the movement and to
nullify its inexorable progress to the development section. The
'second ending' of the bridge-passage modulates into E minor
and the measured beauty of the opening theme is heard on the
bass strings. It sinks, step by step, and concludes with a tremolando
bass C. The violins play a modified version of the theme, using
the falling semitone motive, and the violas enter in imitation.:

Ex. 27

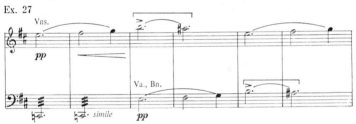

The slow gathering of emotion in this sorrow-laden passage is
achieved by a technical *tour de force*. The screw turns as the rhythms
tighten and the harmonies thicken until the full orchestral climax
is reached. In some commentaries on this section of the movement
we read of the improvisatory nature of this climax. On the con-
trary, Schubert is using the rhythm of his opening theme, Ex.
25 *a*, with all the power at his command. As in the exposition, the
climax yields to the syncopated chord accompaniment. This
dramatic contrast is played twice more, a further example of that
threefold presentation of an idea which made an early appearance
in the *Tragic* Symphony. The heart of the development section is
reached when the orchestra thunders out in unison the main

theme. The abundant creative energy let loose in this movement is a source of wonder. After this powerful orchestral passage there is no relaxation, no sense of exhaustion. By vigorous violin figuration and a new, dotted rhythm in the wind section, the tension is maintained and at the height of the transport the motive *b*, Ex. 25, from the main theme begins to dominate the music. Gradually the storm of emotion subsides; it gathers its forces again, but finally, with pathetic phrases on flute and oboe, it passes. A constructional device of Schubert's, already mentioned, is found at this point: the opening theme is omitted and he starts his recapitulation with the figurative string accompaniment and the cantilena on oboe and clarinet.

Apart from the change necessary to introduce the second theme in D major, the recapitulation is regular, and the effective bridge-passage is repeated to introduce the coda. A final tribute must be paid to the composer for this supremely moving and eminently fitting epilogue. Often in past work he has composed a rousing page or two to conclude his first movements; in fact, his sketch shows that he originally intended to finish this movement in B major. But how unsuitable any change into the major key, or any brisker tempo, would have been at the end of this movement, which Alfred Einstein has called 'an incomparable song of sorrow'! Instead, the motive of the opening theme, modified as in Ex. 27, returns and re-establishes the poignancy of the development section. It gives way to a repetition of the three opening notes alone, played over one of the most wistful cadences in music. The coda, by maintaining the sublime quality of all that has gone before it, concludes a movement which is without flaw.

The *andante con moto* is in the unusual key of E major – unusual, that is, for a symphony in B minor; but, as already mentioned, Schubert's original idea was to end the first movement in B *major* and this makes the choice of key for his next movement more understandable. It was not a favourite key of Schubert's, but two of his slow movements – this one and that in the String Quintet – are in E major and each of them is a supreme example of his art. The drama, lyric beauty and the emotional depths of the first movement are present at the same intensity in the slow movement and to them is added a poetry and a direct appeal to the listener which Schubert rarely equalled in later work.

A short prelude – chords on horns and bassoons supported by a descending pizzicato scale on the basses – and the strings, with the texture of a string quartet, announce the main melody. That the prelude is anything but a simple device to open the movement becomes clear as the *andante* proceeds, for Schubert treats it as an important and integral part of his main theme. Towards the end of the section, violins and bassoons add an arching, cadential phrase and this, too, assumes an important role later on. A fortissimo passage of a processional nature interrupts the meditative mood for a moment, but this is resumed; the preludial bars lead to a pianissimo close on a chord of E major. As it dies away we hear a sustained G sharp on the first violins; the phrase rises an octave and falls slowly through a chord of C sharp minor in which key a soft, syncopated accompaniment begins to throb on violins and violas. The use of syncopated figures is a marked feature of the two movements of the *Unfinished* Symphony and at this point they introduce a magical episode. The clarinet breathes its cantabile melody, gradually ascending to a high A: Schubert's uncanny sense of colour and his love of transition between minor and major modes are nowhere more exquisitely embodied than in the bars which follow:

Ex. 28

The oboe continues the melody in D flat and it ends with a two-bar cadential phrase; this is repeated first by the flute and again by the oboe, each of the threefold presentations with a lessening dynamic until the last, which is marked *ppp*. On this hushed cadence the full orchestra burst in playing the clarinet melody fortissimo with a striking counterpoint on the strings. The tumultuous unleashing of forces continues and the texture becomes even more elaborate until the passage concludes suddenly on a chord of D minor. These abrupt orchestral contrasts characterise this Symphony and unify the varied moods and procedures too; this precipitous end to an orchestral fortissimo, followed at once by the subdued, syncopated chords of the second subject, recalls similar moments in the first movement.

Schubert is preparing for the return of his opening music and he does so by two episodes of exquisite poetry. They are not essential to the form or balance of the movement, although they are part and parcel of it; they are the outcome of a transport of lyrical feeling expressed by details of orchestration such as music had never known before. The first is a simple canon between bass strings and violins of such beauty that wonder is awakened every time it is heard:

Ex. 29

The passage is repeated and concludes in C major. The woodwind enters and above a continually throbbing C major chord, oboe, flute and clarinet in turn utter a soft questioning phrase; each is answered by the horn, dropping through an octave on E which is played with a dynamic which lessens from *p* to *pp* and then to *ppp*. The horn establishes the keynote to the ear; the transition to E major is unconventional yet more satisfying than any conventional cadence:

Ex. 30

The recapitulation, as in the first movement, is regular except that the second subject is in A minor. Towards the end both the preludial bars and the arching figure on the strings are given an extended treatment and eventually they reach a full close in E major. The coda to this movement is, in the opinion of many critics, the supreme achievement of the whole work. Once again we are moved to profound admiration that Schubert's perception has enabled him to conclude a flawlessly conceived movement with a section which maintains, and even rises above, the standard of the whole *andante*. From the E major cadence, the violins hold the note B and we hear again the rise and fall of the solo phrase which introduced the second subject. But the fall of the E major chord is interrupted by a chromatic note, C natural. It introduces the opening song-theme played on clarinets and bassoons, supported by the bass trombone, in A flat; the cadential phrase is heard on the inner strings and brings the episode to an end in that key. Once more the solo phrase soars on the violins and again a chromatic note, C flat, breaks the sequence of the common chord of A flat. The C flat is interpreted as B and the song-theme, on flutes, clarinets and horns, is heard, for the last time, in E major; the movement ends in a mood of serenity, with the soft, rich colour of the full orchestra sustaining the E major chord until at last it sinks into silence.

Schubert's sketches for the Symphony, in piano score, include a third movement, marked *allegro*, which was outlined from start to finish. A sixteen-bar melody, headed 'trio', was also written down. He began to score the movement in fair copy, completing the first page only and starting the second; at this point his full score finished. The scherzo is in B minor and opens boldly with a unison theme for full orchestra. It is no more possible to say what the movement would have become than it is in the case of the corresponding movements in the two previous sketched symphonies, although if Schubert's sketches for the first two movements of the *Unfinished* Symphony are put beside the final versions as we have them, it is possible to see the kind of alterations he made, whereby the first, almost commonplace, ideas are completely transformed. Thus it is a dubious theory which holds that Schubert abandoned his scherzo because he sensed its inferiority and was dissatisfied with it. It may be so, but a stronger possibility is that, had he finished the scherzo, it would have been a worthy successor to the preceding two movements.

The Great C Major Symphony

The manuscript score of Schubert's Symphony in C major is a stout volume of 130 leaves. At the head of the first page the composer has written the date 'March 1828', which simply tells us when he began to write in fair copy the full score of a completed sketch. We cannot be sure how long he had been working on the Symphony, but he himself referred to it, presumably as a finished work, in a letter of 21 February 1828. After his death the score, together with most of his other unpublished manuscripts, passed into the possession of his brother Ferdinand.

Some ten years later, on New Year's Day, 1839, the score was seen by Schumann who, visiting Vienna, called on Ferdinand Schubert. It was owing to Schumann's warm advocacy of the Symphony that it was finally performed (in a cut version) at a Gewandhaus concert in Leipzig, on 21 March 1839, conducted by Mendelssohn. A year later the Leipzig firm Breitkopf & Härtel published the orchestral parts and, at the same time, a

pianoforte duet version of the symphony. Subsequent perform-
ances were given in Leipzig and Frankfurt, but elsewhere the
work made slow headway. When the first two movements only
were performed on 15 December 1839 in Vienna, the *Allgemeiner
musikalischer Anzeiger* reported flatly: 'It would have been better
to leave the two movements undisturbed'. In London and Paris
attempts to rehearse the Symphony were unsuccessful and it was
not until April 1856 that London heard it, given in two parts:
the first three movements at one concert, the second, third and
fourth at a concert a week later.

It was not the technical difficulty of Schubert's Symphony that
prevented its acceptance, but the immensity of its conception, the
demands it made on the interpretative powers of both players and
conductor, and on their ability to sense the broad, overall picture
that emerges from the multitude of details – in other words, on
their team-work. For however delectable each of these details may
be if considered in isolation, it is only when they are submerged
into the glorious wholeness of this Symphony that a performance
can successfully establish its majestic structure.

Important constructional features of the composer's work – one
might almost call them his philosophy of sonata-form – are present
at their most elevated in the first movement of the Symphony. To
call the *andante* section which opens the movement an introduction
to the succeeding *allegro ma non troppo* is to use terms which no
longer hold good; the two are indivisible parts of one complete
conception. The main theme is announced at the start of the
andante – the Schubertian prelude which proves to be no prelude
at all but the master-motive of the movement. The theme, a noble
and haunting melody, is played pianissimo by the horns in unison:

Ex. 31

The rise through a major third at the start indicates the pervasive happiness of this Symphony as surely as the minor third
which opened the *Unfinished* Symphony indicated the pervasive
sadness of that movement. Whether deliberately or not, it is the

corner-stone of the whole work. It appears in every single theme throughout all four movements (e.g. Ex. 33, bars 2–3; Ex. 36, bar 2), either rising or falling, either as an interval or as a stepwise progression of the three notes; it occurs in many of the accompaniment figures and it is used with superb effect in several transition passages between important sections of the movements.

An extended and lyrical episode is based on the horn theme, which appears, now with delicate and tuneful variants on the solo woodwind, now with the full power of the orchestra. At the heart of the episode we have the first hint of another thematic figure which Schubert used as a unifying factor in the work: another character, so to say, which appears in all four scenes of the drama. It is an ascending scale in a dotted rhythm and it introduces a series of rich, harmonic diversions in various flat keys. The dynamic rises to a fortissimo reference to the main theme, but this quickly dies away and instead of the expected peroration, oboe and clarinet breathe the theme, with a charming triplet counterpoint on the strings. The extended phrases which broaden the close of the melody are very clear examples of Schubert's incomparable song-technique momentarily taking over. A quickly mounting excitement rises in the orchestra which hardly needs, in addition, the unjustified accelerando given to it by some conductors; it finishes on a full orchestral chord of C major and the *allegro ma non troppo* section of the first movement begins. Schubert's subsidiary, energetic theme is played by strings and trumpets, with triplet chords on woodwind and horns linking its repeated appearances. The composer altered this theme (greatly strengthening it by his simple changes) after the movement was finished; his manuscript shows the enormous number of revisions made necessary by this example of 'second thoughts'. The theme is based on the tonic-dominant idea mentioned earlier in connection with the Third Symphony. The dotted rhythm, on ascending and descending scales, echoed between bass and treble, makes its definitive appearance and the fleetfooted music is intoxicating to hear. It concludes with a sustained, fortissimo C major chord on the full orchestra from which the strings brusquely modulate to E minor for the second subject. On this occasion Schubert does not write one of his enchanting melodic themes, but continues to exploit the pattern of contrasting duple and triple rhythms. The closing phrases have a typically wistful air and these, later in the movement, are enhanced by very original harmonic touches. The varied components which go to the making of his second subject, including the arpeggio figure which is so important a part of the accompaniment, are all used to build a passage of growing tension. The key of E flat is established and in this new tonality an episode of arresting power follows – a hymn to intellectual beauty and one of the two most celebrated passages in the whole work. A pattern is constructed on the string orchestra, made from elements of the second subject, theme and accompaniment, and against this delicately conceived background the trombones, softly, but in a highly authoritative manner, play a motive derived from the horn theme which opened the movement. Apart from the majesty of the passage as sheer sound, the glancing tonal changes, A flat minor, B major, E minor, G minor and E flat major, are extraordinary and their complex colours lend a radiance to the final emergence of G major for the orthodox close of the exposition section.

The development is wholly Schubertian yet unlike any other in the whole of his work. It is all of a piece, an unbroken surge of inspired writing. From the G major chord at the conclusion of the exposition the music turns nonchalantly into A flat major; episodes based on the second subject (a more melodious variant of this rather plain theme) and the rhythmic scale passages alternate and a slow crescendo leads to the inevitable climax. Schubert was apparently seeking to achieve a subtle distinction in the rhythm of these leaping scale passages for they are written in these two different forms:

Ex. 32

It is doubtful whether the ear can distinguish between these, perhaps over-subtle, differences. At the orchestral climax the trombones again play the opening motives of the main theme, this time in triumphant fortissimo tones. A procedure familiar from the many uses of it in the *Unfinished* Symphony leads to an abrupt breaking-off from the fortissimo cadence, leaving the clarinets whispering the triplet chords of the accompaniment. The whole episode is repeated, scored for strings and solo woodwind; the tone is hushed and the effect is magical. A long phrase in A flat, for the bass strings, leads to a cadence in C minor, which suggests the advent of the recapitulation.

In a famous paragraph on Schubert's tonality, Sir Donald Tovey drew attention to the composer's unerring judgement where the arrival of his required key is concerned. Tovey used the recapitulation from the first movement of the Sonata in B flat to illustrate his point; the premature arrival of the tonic key, B flat, is set aside by Schubert and then, with careful preparation, more inevitably brought back. The same judgement is alert in the Symphony movement; the C minor cadence is avoided. The bass phrase is repeated, reaches C minor, and finally C major. This more finely judged return to the tonic key adds to the effectiveness of the start of the recapitulation. It is fairly regular and the chief modification is to present the second subject in C minor. The fresh treatment of its wistful closing phrases lengthens the section considerably. The coda provides further evidence of Schubert's ambitious striving 'after the highest in Art', to use his own words. It is a substantial section containing new and impressive uses of the thematic scale-figure, Ex. 32 (i). The tempo is quickened by a *più moto* marking, but in view of the high-spirited and triumphant nature of the movement, this is justified. At the very end of the coda the orchestra proclaims in full splendour the main theme of the movement.

Structurally the slow movement, *andante con moto*, can be reduced to the following simple plan:

X (A minor): Y (F major): X (A minor): Y (A major).

The episodes, however, are so richly endowed, variant forms so freely lavished on them as they return, the interludes between them so touched with Schubertian poetry, that the listener is hardly aware of this firm, underlying scheme. The style of the first episode is that of a threnody, recalling 'Gute Nacht' at the start of *Winterreise*, or the slow movement of the Piano Trio in E flat. Above the measured tread of the accompaniment, the oboe plays the first subject:

Ex. 33

A tender phrase in A major serves as an epilogue and then, by the use of the two thematic motives marked *x* and *y*, Schubert builds a stormy passage full of restless, almost fevered, strife. The emotion subsides and a cadence in A major is reached. The bass strings move down through a major third – a beloved device of the composer's – so that the music modulates to F major. The melody of the second episode follows upon the orchestral storm of the previous passage like balm to the senses; the short, contrapuntal phrases which adorn its progress add to its charm. The texture, woven from these strands, remains transparently clear and the orchestral colouring is subdued. Towards the end of the section there is a short interlude of idyllic beauty springing spontaneously from Schubert's imagination and thrown in here for good measure. Constructed on his tonic-dominant idea, the lovely phrases are heard first on clarinet and bassoon, and then on the oboe; the accompaniment consists of syncopated chords on the strings, with delicate shakes, off the beat and clashing with the harmony, played by the cellos:

Ex. 34

Schubert's imaginative power is at its summit. We hear the F major melody on the high registers of the woodwind – ethereal and remote – and it ends on a dominant seventh in C major. There follows a passage, a dozen or so bars in length, which is the most famous in the whole of his symphonic output. Schumann singled it out for comment; he wrote: 'There is one passage . . . where a horn is calling as though from a distance, that seems to me to have come from another sphere. Everything else is hushed, as though listening to some heavenly visitant hovering around the orchestra.' Schubert's horn calls on G, while the strings propose the remaining notes of various dominant sevenths in which G is successively the root, the fifth and the seventh; these eventually resolve in A minor for the return of the opening episode.

The oboe theme is now decorated with rhythmical calls on trumpet, horns and strings and these decorations bring about a more elaborate texture for the recapitulation of the whole section. A figure based on *x* in Ex. 33 begins to assume great prominence; it is akin to the scale passage of the first movement (Ex. 32) and, in conjunction with the rhythmical calls, an overpowering climax is inexorably shaped; at its height the full orchestra plays a diminished seventh chord marked triple forte. This is followed by silence. Soft, pizzicato chords on the strings serve as a prelude for a cello melody derived closely from the main theme of the movement; it is a lovely variant, in B flat. The oboe joins the cello and their duet continues in A minor. Again the cello sings its solo melody, in B flat, and again the oboe joins it, this time guiding the music into A major. It is a touching moment and when sensitively played can draw tears.

The second episode now follows in the key of A major. It is embellished with contrapuntal string figures, exquisitely devised, and the whole section glows with a fresh radiance so that it is as unlike the conventional repetition of classical procedure as it is possible to be. Pizzicato effects, legato phrasings, detached bowings: all manner of string colour is used to lend variety to the harmonic background.

The coda is devoted to the opening theme as quoted in Ex. 33, with an extended use of the phrase *x*. The wistful A major epilogue, with its charming companion-phrase, appears for the first time in the minor key, providing a welcome lyrical touch in the prevailing ostinato rhythms:

Ex. 35

The movement closes with a reference to the four notes of the phrase *y* in Ex. 33. Schubert aimed at a discordant cadence by raising the second two notes a semitone, and no doubt such a device was sufficiently startling to ears in 1828. Today it is simply a pleasantly stimulating touch of colour in the general monotone of A minor.

The third movement, an *allegro vivace*, is planned on the same expansive lines as the preceding movements. It is Schubert's most ambitious, most lavishly wrought scherzo, composed in full sonata-form. There is great variety in all his scherzo-forms, but as a rule they incline either to the figurative, almost non-melodic kind, as in the G major String Quartet, or to the lyrical kind, as in the work which immediately preceded the Symphony in C, the Fantasia in F minor for piano duet. In the scherzo of this Symphony, however, both elements are blended. The virile, rhythmic figure of the opening theme threads the whole movement, hardly ever silent; it is developed as a main subject: it is used as an accompaniment figure: in one delicate episode it initiates a fugato pattern of great appeal. But the melodious passages which spring spontaneously from the ceaseless dance of this figure are among the most attractive in the whole work. Two of the more important of these tuneful excursions are examples of Schubert's tendency to compose waltz-themes during the course of a scherzo; it is as if the regular three-in-a-bar beat had awakened his memories of those sociable evenings, the Schubertiads, during which he had improvised dance-music for his friends. The first of them constitutes the second subject of his scherzo:

Ex. 36

The charm of this melody is enhanced by its close imitation
played at two bars' distance by the cellos. The rise and fall of the
arpeggio figure in the theme persists on the strings, striding
through various keys till the cadence, in G major, is reached. As
in the first movement, Schubert starts his development section by
a shift into A flat, and deploys the various aspects of his opening
theme with tremendous energy. A chromatic twist and the music
modulates into C flat major for the second of his melodic interludes, a delicious, sublimated Viennese waltz, with an unashamed
waltz-accompaniment. The lyrical musing, however, is brushed
aside by a return to the main theme, with a long development of it,
and of the ranging arpeggios from the theme quoted in Ex. 36.
The start of the exposition cannot be pinpointed among the varied
appearances of the rhythmic theme, but eventually we reach the
recapitulation of the second subject, Ex. 36, in C major. The course
of the music is then regular to its close.

The trio is in A major, a long-drawn and expansive dwelling on
one of Schubert's most luxuriant themes. A characteristic of this
theme shows how indestructibly Schubert's melodic writing is
rooted in his flexible, harmonic language. The cadence at the close
of the trio melody is redeemed from any touch of mediocrity by
the use of mediant harmony (first inversion of a C sharp minor
chord) (i). The repetition of the cadence, a little later, takes ad-
vantage of this chord, now in root position, first to reject, then
to accept (ii), a modulation into the *key* of C sharp minor:

Ex. 37
(i)

(ii)

The accompaniment is unusually full; for most of the time the whole orchestra is kept going to amplify the background. Any relaxation in the tempo of this trio is to be deplored; the music is as near to sentimentality as anything which Schubert ever wrote, but played at the required *allegro vivace*, it never crosses the boundary between genuine and spurious emotion.

The final movement of Schubert's Symphony, one of the colossi of the whole orchestral repertory, is an exception to the general rule, mentioned earlier, that the main theme or themes appear at the very outset and form the basis of the development section. But Schubert's three thematic motives, which make up the first subject, are all drawn upon in the course of the movement, caught up into the fierce energy of creation which mastered him in the composition of this finale. Today such words as these are suspect; no doubt the impression we get in listening to this movement, of its being composed in a white heat of inspiration, conflicts entirely with reality, with the cold control which Schubert exercised at his desk. The facility of the writing, however, its endless resourcefulness and the volcanic power which at times is let loose in the orchestra, all this is undeniable.

Ex. 38

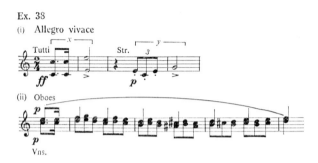

After the motives *x* and *y* in (i) have initiated the movement, there is a long and thrilling passage based on (ii) played over a dominant pedal. Towards the end of the section we hear an astonishing prediction of the second subject, astonishing for a reason which can be considered below. It is followed by the rising and falling scale-figures, with a dotted rhythm, which have recurred in previous movements, and the section ends in G major. After two silent bars, horns and clarinets play four minims on D natural which herald the second subject, one of Schubert's supreme ideas, a glorious and self-sufficient melody and yet capable, as he showed later, of the profoundest intellectual treatment. The theme suggests a sudden, spontaneous inspiration and his manuscript score, at this point, seems to confirm the impression, yet the four minims whereby it was introduced, and which form so dominating a feature of the theme itself, were heard announced in the midst of the first subject material. This fact, together with an extensive use of the motive *y* as an accompaniment figure for the second subject, gives an impressive sense of unity to the whole finale.* Schubert's second subject concludes with an after-phrase which is quoted here:

Ex. 39

---

* The four minims, which become increasingly important as the finale proceeds, are a 'cyclic' use of the phrase *y* in Ex. 33, from the slow movement.

The simplicity of its outline is deceptive; Schubert was instantly aware of its potentialities and his intellectual power – that gift of yielding all his creative impulses to the inherent possibilities of a series of notes – is to be seen at its highest in the development section and in the coda.

The second subject is repeated, without preparation, *on* rather than *in* B major. Schubert achieves the same effect here as he did in his setting of Goethe's wonderful poem *An Schwager Kronos*; in that song Schubert's sudden shift into another key brings to mind the rapidly changing vistas glimpsed during a rise through Alpine scenery. It is as if we had caught sight of a sheltered valley in the midst of sunlit mountain ranges. The leaping scale-figures add to the sense of unbridled motion; the tension increases to a climax and the phrase quoted in Ex. 39 is proclaimed by the full orchestra marked triple forte. The gradual decline in dynamic is achieved in a long-drawn passage; the rhythm of the opening figure x (in Ex. 38 (i)) points the cadences while the descending intervals of the after-phrase eventually resolve on to a chord of G major to mark the end of the exposition. The cellos retain the note G with tremolo bowing: it sinks to F, then to E flat. In this new key the development begins.

Delicate, song-like phrases derived from the second subject are played by the woodwind. They are given imitative treatment and pass through A flat and D flat, finally reaching C sharp minor. The sense of swift movement never relaxes, for the strings continue to play the lilting measure of the scale-figures. In the new key the imitative treatment of the theme is repeated, but scored for the strings with tremolo bowings. In both cases we have a further example of Schubert's threefold presentation of favourite material. The C sharp minor passage is repeated in E minor, and again in G minor. A wonderfully impressive, new treatment of the second subject forms the central climax of the development section. The four minims which herald the theme are thundered out on bass strings, horns and trombones; soon they are joined by the violins, playing the theme in canon. An admirable technical feature in this section is the appearance of a descant-like counterpoint placed off-centre, so to say, its accents at odds with those of the theme it accompanies.

An unconventional cadence in G major is reached and the

sudden sound of the rhythm of x from Ex. 38 announces the recapitulation. The music thins down to repeated G's. An F natural is added to the G and all seems ready for the return of C major for the opening theme. But the incalculable Schubert resolves the F, not on to the expected E, but on to E flat. Abruptly the opening figure is played, fortissimo, in E flat and the recapitulation begins in that completely unexpected, entirely unconventional, but triumphantly justified, key. The first part of the recapitulation is shortened slightly and modified to allow the second subject to appear in C major. The close is reached in that key with, once again, the cellos playing the tremolando C natural.

The mighty coda which ends the Symphony shows Schubert in his freshest, most imaginative vein: no conventional fanfares or decorations of the chord of C major will suffice, although both these elements are woven into the general fabric to enhance the triumph of the closing pages. The two hundred or so bars of the coda constitute another development section, nearly as long, in fact, as the one at the heart of the movement. The cello phrase sinks through a third, as before, concluding in A major. Ambiguous harmonies clothe the thematic figures of the main theme; the radiance gathers brightness until, at its height, the second theme sounds joyfully in E flat major. This passage is repeated and we hear those heartwarming strains in F, G and, finally, C major. At this climactic point the four minims are played on the keynote, C, sforzando, by strings, horns and bassoons in unison. These anvil-strokes are heard again and again in the course of the final moments of the Symphony; between each of them the phrases of the second subject soar on wave after wave of brilliant orchestral tone. The chromatic harmonies give way to a blaze of C major and with a final reference to the rhythms of the opening theme the movement ends.

Schubert never heard this Symphony performed. The orchestra of the Vienna Gesellschaft der Musikfreunde, for whom it was composed, found it beyond their powers; he recalled it, offering the earlier symphony, No. 6, in the same key. Before this could even be put into rehearsal, he died.

For the Sake of Completeness

Antonio Salieri, when asked about the lad Schubert's progress, replied: 'Der kann alles' – 'that boy can do everything', and he continued: 'he composes operas, songs, quartets, symphonies and whatever you want.' The reference to 'symphonies' is interesting. The date of Schubert's Symphony No. 1, October 1813, coincides with his leaving the college, so that Salieri's words must concern earlier attempts than this. We have no record of how many symphonies the lad composed before 1813, but from the competence and assurance in No. 1, we can deduce that it was not his first symphonic essay even if documentation be lacking. A fragment of one of his earliest efforts to write a symphony has survived, together with two other relics, an overture and a string quartet. O. E. Deutsch catalogues these juvenilia as 996–8; his attributed date – 1812 – is, however, too late. The handwriting of the three juvenile manuscripts is very different from that in other manuscripts which have survived from 1812, being altogether more childish in appearance. The symphony and the overture are in full score. They are both in D major and in each case an *adagio* introduction, 3/4, leads to the *allegro* in common time. They have several ideas in common, and a study of the two pieces suggests that the symphony was derived from the overture.

Both fragments are all that survive of larger manuscripts, and in the case of the overture, of a possibly completed work. One feature of the two scores, which suggests a schoolboyish origin, is that on a few pages Schubert has drawn his bar-lines through the score with a ruler, a refinement which he dispensed with as soon as the business of writing down music became more a routine matter. The heading on the second manuscript is simply 'Sinfonie'. The arrangement of the instrumental staves is unorthodox, indicating that the lad was unfamiliar with the standard practice of the day. Reading downwards, the instrumental staves are: timpani, horns, bassoons, oboes, clarinets, flutes, strings and trombones. The *adagio* begins with an orchestral flourish. It is followed by a pleasantly lyrical passage, scored for strings and oboe, echoed by flutes and horns, which hints at the composer's quality. The music ends on a half-close in D major. The *allegro* makes a promising start. The main theme is vigorous, a decorated, rising major third, supported by striding figures on the bass strings. It is remarkable, too, to find even in this very early work an attempt to introduce motives from the *adagio*, integrating them with the material of the *allegro*. Two and a half pages of score (five sides) have been preserved: the *adagio* is eleven bars in length; nineteen bars of the *allegro* follow.

Three controversial matters concerning Schubert's symphonies should be briefly considered for the sake of completeness. The first is a question which is periodically raised: is the Entr'acte in B minor, which Schubert included in the incidental music for the play *Rosamunde*, the missing finale of the *Unfinished* Symphony?* It is doubtful if this possibility would have occurred to musicians had the entr'acte been in any key other than B minor. But it has occurred too widely to be summarily dismissed. The first record of an association between the two works is found in connection with an actual performance, when the entr'acte was played as a finale to the *Unfinished* Symphony. This was at a Crystal Palace concert on 19 March 1881. In the programme notes Sir George Grove wrote: 'We have ventured to add a movement from the *Rosamunde* music, which ... may be found to form a not in-appropriate completion to the unfinished work.'

The fine quality of the entr'acte and certain thematic links between it and the first movement of the symphony are in favour of the proposition. We could also add that since Schubert removed the unfinished page of the scherzo from his manuscript score he may have removed all, or part of, a finale on the same occasion. He was certainly pressed for time in the composing of the *Rosamunde* music and a spare orchestral movement would have come in very handy for the punctual completion of his task. The other side of the argument can be given in the words of a critic who attended the 1881 performance: 'Fine and gorgeous as this remarkable music unquestionably is, it wants the necessary verve, dash and gaiety to form a fitting conclusion to a symphony.'

* cf. Gerald Abraham, 'Teasing Riddle of the Unfinished', *Daily Telegraph*, 10 February 1968.

The second controversial issue concerns the Sonata for piano duet in C major (D.812). This was published by Diabelli in 1838 as Op.posth.140 and given, by the publisher, the title 'Grand Duo', by which name it is still miscalled. Schubert's autograph, an exquisitely written manuscript, has been preserved and is unequivocally headed 'Sonate fürs Pianoforte zu 4 Händen'. It was composed in June 1824 at Zseliz in Hungary, during the period when he was engaged as music master to Marie and Karoline, the daughters of Johann, Count Esterházy. The orchestral aspects of this duet-sonata are to be found in all Schubert's pianoforte music to a greater or lesser degree; to a greater in such works as the *Wanderer* Fantasia and the Fantasia in F minor for piano duet; to a lesser in the short impromptus and *Klavierstücke*. It is accordingly a little difficult to see why the C major Duet Sonata has been singled out and given the distinction of being considered a possible symphony-in-disguise. Schumann seems to be the first important figure who stated in print his belief that it was so, and he has been followed by other more or less eminent people.

It is true that Schubert sketched his symphonies in piano score, but if he did so, he headed the sketches 'Symphony', he noted down throughout the sketches details of orchestration, and, naturally, he paid no attention to the limitations imposed by the ten fingers. None of these factors are true of the manuscript score of the Grand Duo, which was intended to be a work for the pianoforte, so conceived and so written down.

The work has been scored for orchestra. The first version was made by Joachim and performed on 9 February 1856. Other, more colourful versions have been produced in this century. They all prove conclusively how groundless the theory is, for the work loses far more than it gains in its orchestral guise, and betrays only too obviously its pianistic conception.

Schubert was on holiday with his friend Johann Michael Vogl in the summer of 1825; in July and August they spent some weeks in Gmunden and Gastein. While he was in Gmunden, the composer began to write a symphony. The work is referred to as the 'Gastein' or 'Gmunden-Gastein' Symphony and although no trace of a completed symphony from those days has been found, it was given by Deutsch a place in his Thematic Catalogue and stands there as D.849. Did it ever exist as an independent work, the manuscript being subsequently lost without trace? If all the documents relating to this symphony – letters, memoirs, diary-extracts, and records from the archives of the Gesellschaft der Musikfreunde – are carefully considered *as a whole*, they point to the conclusion that the sketches made in 1825 at Gmunden and Gastein eventually became the great C major Symphony of 1828. This cannot be asserted, as definitely proved, but it is highly probable and adequately interprets all the facts – as no other theory does.

The matter is made unnecessarily complicated if it is combined with the previous theory and the conclusion drawn that the Duet Sonata in C major may be the 'Gmunden-Gastein' Symphony. Adherents of this theory claim that Schubert, while at Gmunden, began to orchestrate the Grand Duo. Against this wild theorising we can place Schubert's own words to his brother Ferdinand. He said firmly on one occasion that he would far rather compose a new piece than arrange or orchestrate an old one. There are some grounds for taking seriously the previous three matters, but none for this last one. Yet it lingers on and is encountered from time to time in unexpected places. One can only hope that Max Planck's fine words may hold good where this theory is concerned: 'Truth never conquers, but its enemies die out.'

When one considers the beauty, the vibrant life, the spiritual radiance of Schubert's last two symphonies, and remembers that he never heard a note of them, and that when he died, as far as he knew, they died with him, certain words of J. B. Priestley come to mind. He wrote them in connection with Scott Fitzgerald, but they apply with equal force to Schubert:

And if no rumour of his ultimate triumph has ever reached his spirit, if nothing could be known to him after his unhappy time had run out, then there is indeed no pretence of justice in the Universe.